"To read Mark Goodwin's poems of rock and grass and sky and the body-mind moving through them is to enter deep place: living, uncontainable – an event not a landscape. His poems are a grounding in minute shifts and experiences: visual reflections become aural echoes, sounds lift off the page into the ear, inferences and possibilities of language are opened up. Meaning pivots on the unexpected. Word and line breaks are subtle levers of time and scale. The page is Mark Goodwin's theatre of transformations. Through the slippage and junctures of language, I find myself out in the open, participant in the tactilities and sights and noises of place. His poems, opening on the page in this locked-down time, gladden the heart."
—Gerrie Fellows (2022)

"Like the landscapes where the poet walks, climbs and watches, language is fractured in these poems. The reader becomes a climber too among words that break and re-form, reflect, scatter and slide in and out of this impressive collection. To read these intensely lyrical and elemental poems is to be transported right inside the moment out of which they were written."
—Janet Sutherland

Also by Mark Goodwin

Else
Distance a Sudden
Back of A Vast
Shod
All Are Lots
Layers of Un
Clause in A Noise
A Book of Dost (with artist Jo Dacombe)
Steps
Tones Fled All (with poet Julia Thornley)
House At Out
All Space Away and In
Rock as Gloss
Portland: a Triptych (with poets Tim Allen & Norman Jope)
Lake-Skin As Eye
Moor (with artist Dominique Cameron)
Erodes On Air
The Long Silences (with artist Mark Spray)
to 'B' nor as 'tree'
Of Gone Fox
Is (with photographer Nikki Clayton)

Mark Goodwin

At

Shearsman Books

First published in the United Kingdom in 2024 by
Shearsman Books Ltd
PO Box 4239
Swindon
SN3 9FN

Shearsman Books Ltd Registered Office
30–31 St. James Place, Mangotsfield, Bristol BS16 9JB
(this address not for correspondence)

www.shearsman.com

ISBN 978-1-84861-841-1

Copyright © Mark Goodwin, 2024.

The right of Mark Goodwin to be identified as the author
of this work has been asserted by him in accordance with the
Copyrights, Designs and Patents Act of 1988.
All rights reserved.

Acknowledgements

The poems in this collection, or versions of them, have been previously published in the following magazines, books & blogs, to whose editors I am grateful:

Back of A Vast, Shearsman Books, 2010; *The Clearing*, *Gogarth South*, rock-climbing guidebook, *Ground Up*, 2015; *Long Poem Magazine*; Longbarrow Press's blog; *Molly Bloom*; *Poetry Wales*; *Raum*; *Reliquiæ*; *Shearsman* magazine; *Tears in the Fence*; UK Climbing's *Crag Notes*.

Versions of 'for this ride' & 'Ground Horizons Here So Arrived' (originally called 'Companion on White Edge') were commissioned by the Companion Stones Project – companionstones.org.uk – in association with Arts in the Peak & Peak District National Park Authority, 2008.

A version of 'for this ride' is included in *Walking in the Peak District, White Peak East* by Paul Besley, Cicerone Press, 2020.

Cover & back cover photo-poems by Mark Goodwin,
from an original photo by Nikki Clayton.

CONTENTS

for this ride / 9
Ground Horizons Here so Arrived / 11
@ / 15
An Idea of Division @ The Brissons / 17
Below A Chûn Down / 22
Mortals Through Gogarth / 24
Substance & Light @ Grinah Stones / 26
Tawny Calls' Textures, A Brackenclose, A Wasdale / 37
Thoughts of a Rockface's & Pool's Procedures / 48

This One Water Gesture / 52

As a Birch on a Slate Cliff Above a Pool / 58
Issues of Location Between, Birchen & Gardom's / 60
Oak & Tarn, Helvellyn Range & White Moss / 66
Ruined Under Mynedd Mawr / 68
June Emanations, Nantlle Hills / 70
A Pink & A Blue Field & A Form / 78
Snow Thick on Beinn Sgritheall / 84
A Glen Arnisdale & A Gleann Dubh Lochain / 86
Matter / 89

Notes / 96

For Rob

who minds
mountains &
rivers' **ways**

for this ride

come out
　ward hear
　　heath
er on air
　step
　　on g
　rounded c
loud let
　soul rotate
　　as hori
　　　zon
　walk sky
wards

Ground Horizons
Here so
A(i)r()rived

Any audience is incidental.
—Ted Hughes

moors are a place where
earths & heavens may

merge

vertigo-ground where far
horizons swirl

here

so here is a there
and so a never

is

arrived

at

.

without compass nor
guide
stoop heather is brown

cloud

      and cloud a low white
              vague
        swelling to smudge

            directions

                .

                    leaning stone
                  torqued so north

       south west & east have
                    been ripped

                      .

            from their magnet

          and the cross of
   height-with-width is ask

                  ew

                    .

          blocks twisted where

        what's written gets s
         plit across surfaces

        a top block holds a

                    .

              solution

                    .

pocket so a pool

of condensed cloud may reflect
vapour or a human

.

face

.

or

.

to put
it an

other
way a

.

hol

.

low in solid rock filled
with water skinned by an

image

of sky or some passing
traveller's in

.

quiry

future sure & faint as
moor-mist

as solid As

gritstone ground
down by un

imaginable cogs
of occ

luded

air

a world's
verti

go-grounds hold

on

to

sk

y

wards a

a's in
definite

sud

den drop

thisness
circled

that

a convo
lution a

then

lands an
imag

space con
tained at

cealed

ined min
iature bod

(s)(c)ent
re

y on
a lip

a pin
fold for

of a
sl

stray lo
cations

it at an

that

other

north east
ern curve

wise clo

sed hiero
glyph's o

that

pulls eye

pen(n)ing

to

An Idea of Division @ The Brissons, A Cape Cornwall, that June 2012

*To move toward is to move away. The origin remains obscure.
I just photographed, in full daylight, a lit electric bulb.*
—Jean Daive

direct due west

a mile off Porth Nanven
two black jagged peaks stitched

to sea by tang
ling threads of surf

grey-fluff-horizon runs through their forms at

∫ height

summits backed
by smudge-white sky ½ a

float ½ flying

∞

from north or
from right to

left three
white tri

angles configured as
hull-&-two-sails

slides

    ∞

as slow certain as some
favoured memory to

wards jagged peaks that dwarf *it*

soon & yet some
life's time away

a yacht will reach
a first peak &

      slip out
        of sight

behind

    ∞

a   yacht's   cargo is
my   eyes   it

hoists   a   flag of
dreamt   space   across

    ∞

that yacht
is white roofs

configured to float and
pass

roofs to catch
wind & roof to

push
down on deep

∞

as the white yacht pass
es towards & then

behind the black rocks 2

sudden white specks
of gannets drop

1 , 2

surf flares in
quick succession de

ton(at)e 2 crisp instants
of silence

∞

its mast will

poke out from

the ridge of

the south

ern peak then

the white tri

angle of its

first sail will

get bigger &

bigger un

til the second

sail & finally

the whole

hull are clear

ly seen slow

ly slid

ing due

south or

from

right to

left un

∞

till   er &

hand   &

eye

∞

a white yacht is gone
behind a black triangle of rock

a white yacht appears
between two black peaks

a white yacht again
slowly disappears so( )on

Below A Chûn Down,
A West Penwith

In a field just an other

side of a granite
dyke, a pacing bull

is a zawn. Time

now is hollow; is
a cave of male

cattle. A zawn
is bellowing;

bull-rumble
roils & rolls through

a Cornish soil up
through my feet.

A bull-zawn is full
of sea-foam, is burst

-ing to bang against
a coast; to send

a sizzling froth
of ancient moments.

Above a pacing
bull: on a moor

a granite mushroom,
called Chûn Quoit,

fattens time between
its stones; is fit

to burst. Below
a bull, towards

a coast, Morvah
church retracts

its horns; slips
its shape of place

& time through

shiny sea-mist & salty
drizzle. Disappears.

May 2006

Mortals Through Gogarth
procedureless version

belay life
hold her line
I placed as gargoyle or
angel guttering attention
or is it praying?
South Stack's lighthouse pokes out
from behind, out from a side
of a small conical mountain headland
headland hung on sea
whitest tinfoil-like but fluid instant
crinkled electric glass-lensed light here
& gone like one tick projected
from a clock
gapped ageless
until again tiny bright prick through grey time
& grey space
I'm tied
to quartzite via nylon & alloy
I belay
pay out some thin continuous currency of ropes
as she climbs above me
I am framed by ridge & arête
in a niche
at my back vertical ground (landedge)
horizontally deep & opaque
in front of me a stupendous drop of sea's horizontal
terror-clear-calm
sea's grey-gleam film all jiggling crozzle as is
quartzite's craze so ever so slightly
translucent rippling sea-like stillness
close up to my face
there sea solidity
sea's solidities, solidities' seas
Gogarth's rock systems & structures multiply

& divide fractals of fear-peace geologically
written as real
imagined fingers proliferate in cracks
touchings of hands on stone pass on
knuckles lichen fingerprints & salt to
histories' now-passed nows
climbing guidebook writers die
in each other's mouths enchained & on
written cliffs of each other's pages
in space stretched between rock
to my left and to my right
in my crack of frame a raven hangs
flagly black updraft-frilled
shocked *crock!* ruck on air
as speckled-cream-blue-flare of feather
& talons cling-tumbles-attack
peregrine & raven spin
and a limp broken meaty scrap of peregrine chick
escapes crack-like shapes of raven claws to fall
to lost
my frame refers
empty as instant is a never
now is only salted air & airy seaish distances
deaths are alive as flight
soon I will untie nylon knots
(untie nylon from oil from age-compressed
essence of insects) untie
from deep ground
shout from throat through mouth
through air through love to her (through her)
"climbing!"

August 2008

Substance & Light @ Grinah Stones east of Bleaklow, cold spell, February 12th 2013

for Brian & Nikki

  & we
  fain

  tly lit
  and

  we a
  p   pr   oach

  light through
  light we approa

  ch light condensed to
  dark out

  crop gritstone all

  this Ridge
  walk Moor is

  all light tight
  ened to all

        solid

        ities'
        text

        ures

& a
light's col

lected flakes

and a
froth of

light shin
-deep sounds

our snow
steps

~

& light
as wide

ness

and a
grey

light pur
ified sm

ooth as ob
durate

slate hangs soft
ly as sky

-vibration

~

      & light

      as a
      crisp

      mist
      blur

      and
      so

      blur
      crisp

      ly lays
      up

      rights
      down

      beyond
      gone's

      horizontals

      ~

& crink
led threads

of light

& scrunched
light fibres

and so light
fibres form

black heather's pro
trusions through

snow's

frequencies of
whites & infinite

variables
of greys

~

& light
sat still

light alert
light as moun

tain hare
black-tipped

ears grazing
sky's grey

freight &
now-light

as speed light as
beast trans

placing here's vast
connecting to

distance sprinting
on light's white

curves paws ki
         cking up

solidity smudged

~

& now
as an

i and
so   i

touch

slow-rough
-heavy-light

light forged by
gravity pulled

to a whole
hole-less

ness of
stone one

of Grinah's
grit-light ex

crescences a
boulder of

slowed en
ergy scul

pted
i feel it
                s light

silenced solid
grit's frict

ion grazes
a thin

surface/tension
of light on

my palm i
call

skin

~

& light
as sound

light

wound
up in a

grouse-throat now

suddenly thrown
over moor gu

gur gurg gurgles

~

& now
(s)now-light rises

up as
crag-ground

rocks muffled
in snowlight's

white hum we
pick our way

among blocks
of time &

hidden slots of
space we climb

through Grinah's
jumble of fro

zen moments sw
ift as light's

pulse

~

& from

as past lit &
light

stretched &
ground passed and

so from
Grinah's top an

apron of moor
we traversed is

        now

spread out is
diffracted below

        us an

expanse of
light liquid

as sea
yet so

      lid as
      bone un

      der skin

& dar

kened light
as punc

tuating spots

a straigh
t row of

black-block
        grouse-butts proj

ects south-east
wards from

Grinah's base
like ru

ined piles
of a lost

pier reach
ing from

land-rim in
to sea's miles

-high-sky &
fathoms-deep

entwined light &

  &

                                                             &

and just be &
yond a

                                                   &

final out

post moor's &
horizontals

                        &   lit-to-solidities ac

celerate into
Grinah Grain's

water-cut
ruck of

space dis
perse to in

fra grey's
depths

~

& light
as glass as

up

turned bowl of
pink-blue-grey

-purples placed
over us

& world
& light

as Turner's

strokes fuse
ing photons to

quantum bonds
east of us

light lifts

up Ronksley Moor
      's peat-water-grit-&

        -heather-mat
              rix of solar

mem
ories light lifts

          light lifts

this so
slow vi

bration now

speeds it
up sky

          wards spreads

this soli
dity of light

as frail gold
gaseous veils

sepia yet elect

        rick through

        lit air's

grey e( )very-ness

Tawny Calls' Textures, A Brackenclose, A Wasdale, A September 2013

silent Sca

fell printed
flat black a

gainst tink
ling stars &

Brackenclose
hut snug

at Lingmell's
toe in

its drystoned tri
angle of old

& named

oaks & long
wiry hill grasses as

Lingmell Beck rubs and r
ubs and ru

bs trans
parent cent

uries & centuries over roun
ded beck-stones every

             second as

the un
lit hut's

silence holds
its voices tight as

picture frames & book
shelves gently

vibrate with

            some

other time's climbers'
faces hackly

as rhyolite greased
with histories as just

            now as

we lie here slipping
down sleep's slope our

tent pitched among
Brackenclose's oaks as

the hut keeps its keep
sakes empty of any

            one yet full

of intentions spent
on crags & fells and its

windows dark
with hopes just

      now a

      single hoot

          a

      pause and

      now   an

      other hoot but

      doubled each

      tawny call en

      twines with and

      yet un

          winds

      every texture Was

      dale's made

      of as sleep's

      fall stretches

          through

      owls' calls to

        ... to ...

                shape

          ground as

                sound

▲

ke-witt   *hoo-hoo*

some where some
where among

Brackenclose's oaks
and some

where beyond a
mong branches & moss

hoo   *hoo-hooohoo*   among

twigs & dew &
leaves & cob

webs & ri
sing threads of

mouse-scent a

throat
throat

here throat

there
throat

throats

warm under feathers form

air in
to colours for

ears   vi

brate breath in
to dream's f(i)re

quencies for
us fall

ing a
sleep sound

see-ers

▲

at a
distance

The Screes'

cones of rub
ble-stones

are smooth that
close

ness of jag
ged & hard to

tread is at

this

distance soft

as song from some

other

world made
by some other

being's

lungs throat
tongue beak

The Screes

plunge

through Wast
Water's sur

face-version
of them

(selves?) down in

to dark's liq
uid lid

ded by bright

smooth mirror as

listening

      glistens

▲

as
a taw

ny's call
pulls as

some *I* falls
to sleep as

some

tent's fabric gently
rattles as

some

holds on

      Great Gable's Needle Ridge

polished

by rivers of
hands & feet

gleam

weather's grease as
my finger

skin slips but

just grips as

my mountain
boots' soles lose

one world's

friction to
gain cloud

& air's
ground

less depth but

I still cling as

some

owls'
sounds

condense on
my fall

ing a
sleep form

▲

every sound Was
dale's made

    of

        is was as

        much

        as now

    ▲

Lingmell's summit is

made

of solid lit
mist & see

through stone ringing

gleam as

sunshine strikes
through cloud as

our feet press and
ground quietly re

sounds steps as
if sleep was

wide bright as

just

beyond Ling
mell Crag's long

drop

Piers Gill's black
gash like an im

print from some
letter dropped and

lost from

some god's
alphabet a

llows

water's pass
age as

Scaffel Crag's ob
duracy dissolves

among water's
dancing

molecules water's

form as
steam as

Scaffel Crag's names   &
buttresses & slabs   &

pinnacles & flakes   &
ascensionists' lines   &

arêtes & cracks &
constructs loom

through faint sounds
of histories'

mist its
moist hiss as

people's sleep forms
patterns on a

mountain hut's
walls as a

warenesses re

solve soul-noise

    as

    owls w

    ake

                                 sound sound
                                   wakes owls

Thoughts of a Rockface's & Pool's Procedures
a The Brand,   a Charnwood,   a Leicestershire

a stepped-on slate slab clanks
as it rocks
         a stepped-on slate slab clanks
           as it rocks Swithland's houses beyond here hunch
    jagged greyblue cracks on the ground they sprout from and
    ripples crossing a pool will mingle with again when
    circles dibbed by fish-mouths

             a moorhen divides her mind
               in reeds ice grinds slate   reflected

[vertical text: in smooth water walls / algae-swirled fingers / & feet have written / lines up these slabs — with mirrored reflection]

                      with letters of crimps & smears

         sun shattered on slate faces
            slate fingers clatter
                           climbers clink
a birch on a slate brow   their gear and look up slate's
                           lines **an orange carp slides**
                              through transparent slate

         a slate birch on a brow

a stunted oak grips
a slate cleft
            a cobweb spanning
            slate fangs **a slate voice erodes as bird**
                     song vibrates molecules

                        meadows of moss blobbed
                        on mountains two **stripes of moss across**
                        -foot high
a slate of grief
slate's glee
                              a slate slab
            wobbling with light by a lily clanks

This One Water Gesture

from far
off a

river's run s   wirls s   wells
its wet

sounds through

air here holds
a whole

valley in one

vast wobbling
sonic droplet of

place

a sound-recordist first
p   laces her ear

here at

point one at
this place-sized

droplet's edge

her delicate metal
microphone is

not really

solid it is
wet's image of

solidity list
ening now

a recordist m   oves
her ear through

various un
real & real

p   oints towards
river-source un

til her ear her
here-ness zeros

                             (cl

        o

                             ses

                             in on)

in on one

        in

                             on

                                              one

ri   p   ple's edge so
wide sounds'

mesh simp

lifies to

to
to

one

impos   sible

cryst
al gest

ure

As a Birch on a Slate Cliff Above a Pool
at a *The Brand*, at a Charnwood,
at a Leicestershire, all imagined

it is making
a birch-wish
to sit

on a slate-lip
blue & sharp
above
a deep sky
-drowned pool

it is a cracking
of birch bones
black or white

and a taking
of a birch tree's
green tongues
to sit

with sharp stone
pressing thighs
as sky falls

into hollow water

it is a birch face
striped white & black
and smeared green
to sit

with jagged
blue cracks
& a pain

of cold stone
congealing
in a muscle

in a pool
below snow
as black as
burnt birch
falls

upwards

Issues of Location Between Birchen & Gardom's, Early-May Two-Thousand & Sixteen

        between the grit

stone lips of Birch
en & Gard

om's Edges
        a throat

of ground run
ning roughly north

west from Robin
Hood Farm &

        the asixonenine's Tarmac stripe

a throat of
ground that holds

to south past
ure-squares set

by drystone wall-lines
dark taught dry

        stone cords hold

ing Moor
sides Farm to

    its land   's pallet

to north the throat
of ground opens

        out

to savannahish
moor moss

birches & brist
ly gras

        ses and turns

        due north to

wards borders made
by the minor

road that runs
north-east from

        Corner

stone Farm to
the gap   be

tween Cur
bar's & Bas

        low's Edges

& the Shef
field Road that

        cuts between Yeld

Farm & Yeld
wood Farm and

climbs north
east through

the wooded
cleft between Jack

Flat & Gardom's
crenulated grit

stone shy
on the valley rim

its buttresses beak
ing between

                oaks & birches

▲

with our ruck
sacks full

of kit to
climb with we

seek the top
of Elliott's Buttress

along Gardom's
intricate rim

spring sun gently man
gling amongst new

leafed birches & stun
ted oaks to resolve

on sheep-cropped
grass amongst

gritstone boulders
I have now

indentified where
we are by

descending the edge
to inspect the

        crag from below

we are just
above Moyer's

Elliott's is just
to our south

▲

to east a
throat

of ground rimmed
by Birchen's

petering-out
edge more

guessed than
seen through

        birch-slat

just to west
Gardom's

lovely matt-grey
rough grit gems

          sud

denly that bowl
ish throat of

ground not
holds   but is

          held

in a two
tone   sound

suddenly birches
oaks heather & boul

          ders are

          un

          see   n as sou   nd

the birch-slat br ight
whites & black

          notes but

          si   lent as

a cuckoo's two
drop   lets of ex

         panding gorge

         ous call

         glassily liquefy

ground's solidity &
its seen & smelled

            maze to one

            vibrating vast

            poin   t

Oak & Tarn
Helvellyn Range & White Moss, November 2016

below Nether
most Crag's drift

-crimped rim black

against snow the system
of Ruthwaite

Cove's gills are
frond

                                         or

root
-net letting

dark's flow through
snow's white soil as

Hard Tarn's ice
-sealed oval hangs

laid

on a table
-cloth or

bed

-sheet of snow high
up the cove's

northern gradients silent

but for one

molten segment's

chime as

water blinks

    o

just beyond White
Moss Tarn along

the Coffin Road

    framed by
    cottage window back

    lit by dawn sky
    a winter

    oak's black dance
    of wig

    gling still
    ness and

            a

    moon

    hanging
    on an

    infinite slope

Ruined Under Mynedd Mawr
just after Christmas, as 2017 approaches

                    as now unspools as

breeze through bunched
green needles of reeds

                 these tumbled

cottage-blocks moss
-clotted are speech

               less as bones

and the rippled
llyn a sheet of

distance disgraced
making

            a sky argue

with wobbling
versions of its own

            blue face

and jagged Craig y Berra
its silhouette-crenulations

            a tottering grasp

for space   a   clawing
for pur   chase any

            tiny grip on

[right margin, vertical: i am or the device i am   simultaneous peripheral operation...   carrying is being   tracked by both   online   American & Russian Global Positioning Satellites   while the system that sent]

sky's   cold   smooth
complexion

and the calm
flake-barked wisdom

of these three
winter sycamores guarding

       this empty

       cottage-tomb

their Roman dignity pretty
as history's best

       glinting fabrics

       and poor

poor charming
Mynedd Mawr

(roman   tic little mountain)
gracefully blind as

       stone

       cannot know nor

       hear

swirling scat   tered in grasses or
wri   thing through

moss-muffled ruin
the chat   tering

       gone

June Emanations, Nantlle Hills, 2017

note: *Cwm Silyn* translates as *spawning lake valley*

I.

<u>Whilst Climbing Outside Edge</u>, <u>The Great Slab</u>, <u>Craig yr Ogof</u>
                 addressed to a reader

Cwm Silyn's three llyns below
– smooth blues slight

ly rippled and spat
tered with the day

-star's sparks

my ropes pale
orange & blue
stripe down

wards across grey tuff

ropes as tugged
map-marks on
actual rockscape

simple linear legends rubbing

their passing over
the complex-crinkled

surface of a
solidified aeon

the day-star's force bounces
off the tuff my skin

seeps salt-wet as

    black flies like
    letters fallen
    from a bible twirl

        two ravens throw
        soft slow *kron-n-n-n-nks* from

    one

        to the o

    ther across
    the simmering cwm

I climb on up
the stone's star-heated
rippled hardness drag

ging my smooth map
-line rope-colours

pitch finished I
anchor to the crag
to bring

up my companion tied
in   to the lines' ends   out
of sight below

and beyond the crag-horizon I've

    just cli
      mbed o
        ver

my mouth gummy
with thick spit
I gaze

-guzzle at the sleek
sky-silent llyns reclined
in the level of

spirits

I almost
believe

I could reach
down and lift and tip
up

a big blue sheet to
pour

a deep bubble of water down
my throat and   g   guh   guh

glug a llyn dry

swallowing whole its
light & sil
very fish-glinters

         a sudden high sli

         ding speckle of dark
         -spark swallows lets

         loose gli
                 stening

chips of song across
the cwm's blue

shivering sky-lid

II.

<u>At Summit above Craig Pennant, 734 m</u>
           un-addressed

      pick

ing steps across light-grey clitter
lovely hollow

glug-clun
ks of

        stones rocked

      a geo

logical music folding
an animal's now

ness move
ments in

            to

deep-timed
stone-gong

       sou

               nd

III.

During Return Walk to Road-Head, Lower Slopes of Garnedd-goch
addressed to my climbing partner & a moor's gone gods

moorland wide-writhing under
sky buzzing white with

the spikes of the day-star

 windless air bend
s into warp
 ing walls

of greased rippling glare

distraught ice-bergs of over
-heated full-fleeced sheep bounce
through black-green reeds away

from us ab
   surd fire
-faced spectres we

are heat's terror

and it's our
visions that play

on the mind of the June moor

bog-cotton puffs copy
gauzily the flock   are
little sheep stuck
on straws

and heat's fuzz-shine is

a tremor at   at
om magnified
to this

pressed

smudge of

lenticular space this
material of contorted

moor & spook-forms our

extra-real
faces pull all

this moor's molecular
vibrations   its forms

into our skulls a craze

of temperature-rise crystallises
behind our eyes

        suddenly I hear a *gliggle* now
        ribbon-glisten in a narrow channel
        the pebble-bottom pristine through

        limpid prophecy

        we kneel to this
        transparent angel reclining
        amongst the reeds

we plunge our hands and pull
  up cupfuls and tip

splashes upon us and
laugh a relief-rapture as a clarity
cold-&-smooth as a home

coming until now un

known re
skins our faces with

 flow

  's lo

 ve

A Pink & A Blue Field & A Form
Lodge Farm, Ullesthorpe, December-end 2017

        closest

        to the farm
        house is *home*

barn field

        west from there is

hovel field and

        between these the bridal

                      runs lined

        by a ditch &

        a hedge &
        a few

        ash

           trees

  .

hovel field slopes and
faces

           south-east

a convex that
when

                        covered (as
                        now)

in snow catches

                                    three

o'clock december
sun-slant so

                a pink dome glows

backed
by sky's blue

                                        while

                willows round
                the pond on

                            the brow

        and the isolated ash

just west

                                            strike

horizon-postures

                    lit

                        in

        silence

                .

we stride across

a snow-rosy
crust our

steps

crackle on
light a pink

field holds

persons'
moments

as

                      a hare's

prints tear
in   vis   ib

ility's speed ov
er a frail

ty of water's
solid

      .

my son crouches
down to a

                small snow

less patch
of ground a

        scrape

rimmed with
crin

kled ice its
shallow

soil-hollow
is gloss

y polished
by a body's

        sett

ling heat he
touches

        earth just

this moment ex
posed to

        sky

.

    at   three   or
           there

    abouts   at

december's end when
lit snow lays

           no self

over the slow
ly growing crop

the hedge casts

shadow across
home barn field in

                                  such

                                  a way so a

                                  strider

                                  may

              (on two

              feet or four

              paws)

                                  pass

through the hedge's

                                  gap

from

        hovel field's bubble

of snow-pinked

glow in   to   *home barn*'s

                            vault of

                            charged blue

Snow Thick on Beinn Sgritheall Down to Around 600m, Very Early Spring, 2018

Beinn Sgritheall's ab
rupt snow-g

host   (a season's
     spook soon

up-ground riding   to
        melt)
    above

brown/green mot
tle-slopes & bir ch
-t

  will

    above

hamlet arn Is dale's
hist orical intri cacies its wisps of

  lived   appearing to

day as   day's
solid de tailed

house-shapes st rung a

     long loch

       shore while

Sleat's Sound and
Loch Hourn's

   h a r d f l o w l a p s

                .

                                all

                            as all
                                            ways

                        from sky

                                    to snow's   sc r oll
    down

                                                                    to

                            ground

                                                sounded

A Glen Arnisdale & A Gleann Dubh Lochain, A Spring Start, 2018

as spring's f   orms jell
and sun's   old

est of new

gest

ures un
furls

here

as

               is

  .

Glen Arn
isdale holds

its burn's gli
de in a

fold

made of

past
ure wo

ods &

hills
ide a

fold seam
ingly solid

as an   alm
an

ac's

time see   ms
to be not

ched in mind

a so
ng of

some bird not

thru   sh but
like holds

all this

fold's solids
now

in a fluid

                                 of s
               ad's

                      gl

ee

      .

        at *Gleandubhlochain* (as

        OS have it at a

        round NG 908103)

where a power

line held
up by lit

tle pylons re
lays

the punch
of electrons

one

        mature rowan grows
        ever older in a

ruin of

cottage peopled
by corp

ulent gleaming green

ferns

Matter
Glen Arnisdale & Gleann Dubh Lochain, March 2018

[…] *without human meaning,*
Without human feeling, a foreign song. – Wallace Stevens

[photo by Boz Morris: Nikki on Beinn Sgritheall. Beinn Sgritheall (pronounced *ben skree-huhl*) rises above the hamlet of Arnisdale & the north shore of Loch Hourn. *Sgritheall* is Gaelic for *a scroll*.

After days of snowy & iced ground, after abrupt ups and steep downs, we turn from the mountains' tops … and so we now walk along, we walk a longa gentler un dulating ground down in the glen. The sting of fast-thrust snow specks in the face is already from some other story. Down here in this nestling Glen Arnisdale spring suddenly begins. Sunshine unfurls its newest of oldest gestures. Our rucksacks are smaller, and our boots not so big. We need no crampons nor axes. It is like a well-earned holiday, this warm day, after the early starts for high cold tops. And holy it is as some unidentified bird pours her or his or its voice through and across the loveliness of Glen Arnisdale. This song is nearly thrush, but it is not thrush. And when we see the bird flit from tree to tree … its jizz, its gestures, its motion is not of a bird I know. I then, at that moment, or probably another moment I made or make from memory, at that some moment I remembered – I remember

– how a poet called Peter Riley wrote, writes, will write ... that he felt (feels) something about a place named Alstonefield mattered, mattered so very much...

Such inexplicable matter, and mattering happens for some version of me – here or there – in a Glen Arnisdale

[Photo by Nikki Clayton: Looking west down Glen Arnisdale. The mouth of Loch Hourn, The Sound of Sleat, and Sleat on the Isle of Skye can be just seen in the distance.]

Behind us, as we walk east, is Loch Hourn's mouth, open to The Sound of Sleat. (And beyond the south shore of that slot of sea loch, and its sprung expression of mixed waters – fresh & salt – stands the almost fabled Rough Bounds of Knoydart, tops snow-glossed and east flanks silvered.) In front of us, to east, Glen Arnisdale's wide pasture ends in a tight throat where River Arnisdale is squeezed between rock-knolled hill-ground. And through this throat-gate we pass into Glenn Dubh Lochain, with its two damned reservoirs, its two black lochans, set prettily and smoothly in some newly revealed scape of tangled textures. Spring's sunlight shatters glee gorgeously sad across these dark foils. We try to stalk otters along these lochans' frilly banks, but we see nothing, no signs at all, but I notice how I hope I am watched...

[Photo by Nikki Clayton: In the glen junction, or where Gleann Dubh Lochain bends to the east, looking easterly.]

And further on, and where this hidden glen t-junctions, and where burns merge, and where little pylons carrying power-lines pass, their frames' movements through this place defined by their actually staying still within it – here, at this juncture, there are some ruins. The larger house has been sky-opened, and young rowans grow on the battlements of its crumbling. And the much smaller equally sky-seen & sky-tortured roofless one-roomed cottage to the north-west of the bigger wreck, this residency is occupied by a plant-being, an old thick-trunked rowan … and all four walls of the raw open interior are peopled by glistening green ferns…

I never arrived at

[Photo by Nikki Clayton: Looking south west down Gleann Dubh Lochain, in the direction of the small reservoirs. *Dubh Lochain* is Gaelic for *black lochans* or *tarns*]

this place as much as I never left. The little pylons, and they are little, they are children pylons in comparison to the ones I know in Leicestershire, but they are also mountaineer pylons, their smallness their fury, these beautiful pylons delicate as birches … and the mature rowan growing ever older boxed in its sky-roofed cottage well, my self's (or an other's) really having existed and not existed here or else

      where is as…

      feasible as
      a dance

      of pylons whilst
      a stoic rowan plays

      that dance's tune

      with its buds

      of air

[Photo by Nikki Clayton: ruin & mountain pylons.]

Notes

At was virtually completed by 2020, just before 'the locked-down time', to quote Gerrie Fellows. So, although the book was not published until 2024, it should be placed somewhere between my chapbooks *Lake-Skin as Eye* (The Red Ceilings Press, 2019) & *Erodes On Air* (Middle Creek, 2021).

for this ride

There are (of(f) course) a number of definitions for the word 'ride'. One of these definitions, according to the SOED, is: *Ride / verb. Rest or turn as on a pivot, axle, etc.; fig. rely or depend on something (Foll. by on, upon) b. Extend or project over something; protrude; overlap.*

In 2008 I was commissioned by the Companion Stones Project to collaborate with artist Jo Dacombe ... so, 'for this ride', as well as being in this book is also chiselled into the surface of a gritstone sculpture placed on White Edge in The Peak District. Here's what the Companions Stones website says about the project: *A celebration of the Derbyshire Guide Stoops, Companion Stones is a set of twelve matching stones. Designed by local poets and artists and created by sculptors and masons of the Peak, the stones are of similar stature, volume and material of their compeers. Like the Guide Stoops, each bares an inscription pointing, not to market towns, but towards the future. In so doing they draw attention to the moors, an indicator of the tricky environmental terrain we have yet to navigate.*

Since 2008 the White Edge companion stone has been 'adjusted' by unknown passers-by. On the first occasion it was upturned and rolled off the escarpment! An event that both artist Jo Dacombe & I mark as an essential part of the poem-sculpture's 'journey'. After the sculpture had been hauled back up on to the ridge someone modified its structure in a way we consider massively detrimental (but necessarily also part of its 'journey'). The structure consists of two gritstone blocks, one placed on top of the other. The top block should be slightly rotated and not aligned with the bottom block. However, someone's 'sense of orderliness' has caused them to fix the blocks flush to each other. At some point I'm going to head up there and hopefully manage to un-align the blocks again, unless someone's glued them!

The White Edge companion stone, and the text of its poem, also make an appearance in Paul Besley's *Walking in the Peak District, White Peak East* (Cicerone Press, 2020). As it happens, the photo in Paul's book shows the sculpture in its correct 'rotated' form.'

More info about the Companion Stones Project is @companionstones.org.uk

Ground Horizons Here So Arrived

Any audience is incidental. is from Ted Hughes' poem 'Moors', from *Remains of Elmet*.

The @ sign was originally an invoicing & accounting abbreviation meaning 'at the rate (or price) of'.

Allegedly, the earliest discovered symbol in this shape is found in a Bulgarian translation of a 1345 Greek chronicle, now kept in the Vatican Apostolic Library. We are told that the chronicle features the @ symbol in place of the capital letter alpha "A" as an initial in the word Amen; as yet, it seems no one knows the reason behind it being used in this context. But I rather suspect it *at* least had something to do with 'God'. [Source: Wikipedia.]

'@' of course is now the prime targeting part of digital (email) addresses and has come to be closely associated with @ as 'at' in the sense of 'here' (or is that 'there'?). But where 'here' is exactly is now even more confusing since the advent of the notion of 'cyberspace'.

And apparently, in philosophical logic, '@' is used to denote the actual world (in contrast to non-actual possible worlds). In philosophical logic one can have great fun making possible distinctions such as: "@ is the actual world" versus "@ is the actual world at @". [Source: Philosophy, etcetera.]

> Please do not @just your set. @
> – the poem – does require
>
> the reader/looker/rover to per
> haps squint ... into a distance ..

An Idea of Division @ The Brissons

If I recall correctly, the epigraph is from Jean Daive's *Under the Dome: Walks with Paul Celan*

Mortals Through Gogarth

Gogarth is the name of a tall and extensive area of sea-cliffs on Holyhead Island, between South Stack and North Stack. It is a major climbing venue. The Welsh name Gogarth apparently incorporates the following definitions: promontory, hill, highland, enclosure, step, ledge, terrace.

'Mortals Through Gogarth' in *At* is the procedureless version of 'Mortals Through Gogarth' in *Back of A Vast* (my 2010 book published by Shearsman). The poem in this book is the primary version before the procedure was imposed on the poem in that book. The procedure was two-fold: First certain words were 'gapped' – or s   plit ap   art – and then stanzas were arranged according to a strict line count (in this case an alternation between 2-line and 3-line stanzas).

A version of this procedureless version was published by Ground Up, in their rock climbing guidebook, *Gorgarth South*, 2015.

Tawny Calls' Textures

Brackenclose is a mountain hut owned by The Fell & Rock Club, situated at the head of Wast Water. It was built in the 1930s, and is steeped in climbing & mountaineering history.

Lingmell is a high fell outlying Scafell Pikes & Scafell.

The Screes are famous for the spectacle of their plunge down into Wast Water from the fells of Whin Rigg & Illgill Head.

Needle Ridge is a well-travelled (thus polished) classic mountaineering rock-climb on the fell Great Gable (rather tricky when damp, a condition referred to by climbers as 'greasy').

Scafell Crag is a huge, high rock-climbers' arena – laden with climbs (or lines) ranging from pleasant late 19th Century classics through to modern technical terrors!

Thoughts of Rockface's & Pool's Procedures

Leicestershire Climbs describes the The Brand thus: "Situated in the private garden of The Brand, this crag-like quarry offers some very fine climbing on steep, often perfect slate."

And the guidebook also mentions that: "Before the Enclosures of about 1820, stock used to be driven annually to places on the edge of Charnwood Forest to be marked with the brands of their owners. The Brand was one such place." And goes on to say: "Slate quarrying was a growth industry in the Brand area in the 17th and 18th century. The stone, suitably dressed, was used for headstones (remember this when you climb here), guttering, water troughs, gate posts, drystone walling and flagstones."

I make use of three technical rock-climbing terms in this poem: *line* is another name for *route* or *rock-climb*; *crimp*(ing) is a technique whereby a very thin edge of rock is gripped with the fingertips – by positioning the fingernail phalanges vertically so that the fingers' flat bone-ends can be pressed hard on to the stone rugosity; to *smear* is to place a toe or ball of the foot on an ill-defined sloping foothold, in contrast to *edging*, which is to place a toe or side of the rock shoe onto a distinct lip or edge of rock.

This One Water Gesture

The expression *this one water gesture* was spoken by listener-&-field-recordist-composer Hildergard Westerkamp, whilst being interviewed by composer sound-artist Cathy Lane. (Source: *In The Field, The Art of Field Recording*, Cathy Lane & Angus Carlyle, Uniform Books, 2016).

Issues of Location Between, Birchen & Gardom's

The buttresses on Gardom's Edge referred to in the poem, were named after 1930s pioneer rock-climbers Clifford Moyer & Frank Elliott.

The following is my (somewhat oblique!) introduction to the poem as first published by *Long Poem Magazine*:

'Issues of Location Between Birchen & Gardom's' happens in various places-&-times, at once. In the title, the once is given as 'Early-May Two-Thousand & Sixteen', but the once is an about-to-be for you (or a just-been, if you've already read the poem) as much as it is others' onces upon, beneath and alongside various times' layers & locations' co-ordinates. Essentially the once – the once with a The – is a version of a now in a past-place, and simultaneously the now of experiencing that version, which is the poem's (or map's) happening. This is simply riddle-ish. And this is what a map does – makes a riddle that pretends to be simple. The infinite bits of 3D land-detail are visually abridged through relatively very few 2D drawn lines, then labelled with words. As map-readers we see names, sometimes say their sounds. And as we walk over or climb upon the ground's touchable map, the paper map may make its simple declarations that we choose to believe to know where we are ... or rather we choose to know the simplified declarations' legend(s) to be(lieve) where we are. All the while the land's countless sounds – its grasses rubbing grasses and tapping stones, its leaves' shush in air – these noises that are other than words, these actively fill any vacuum(s) made by our maps' simplifying de(-)positions. Also there are the calls of ultimately incomprehensible creatures. And every now, and every again, abrupt as lightening, the living ground's sound punctures our map. / Note: For useful & aesthetic accompaniment I recommend *OS Explorer OL24, The Peak District, White Peak Area*, 1:25 000 scale. Revised December 2013, reprinted with new cover May 2015. (The new cover depicts a view from the mouth of Thor's Cave.) A representation of Gardom's Edge can be found here: OS Grid Ref: SK 27149 73208. For photographic, diagrammatic and verbal representations of Gardom's Edge (and Birchen Edge also) I recommend *Eastern Gritstone, Froggatt to Black Rocks, The Definitive Guide*, British Mountaineering Council, 2010.

Ruined Under Mynedd Mawr

Mynedd Mawr is a small shapely mountain a few miles due west of Yr Wyddfa in North Wales. Craig y Berra is the mountain's steeply ridged and loose-rocked upper south face.

June Emanations

Outside Edge Route is a *classic mountaineering route of much character*. It was first climbed in July 1931 by Menlove Edwards. This rock-climb is given a traditional grade of Very Difficult (which is actually not difficult at all, by modern standards).

Matter

The epigraph is from Stevens' poem, 'Of Mere Being', from his selected collection, *The Palm at the End of the Mind*.

Thanks

As ever, my thanks to Tony Frazer for at-tending so sensitively to page-space & shape.

Thank you to Jo Dacombe for assisting with some of the very intricate layout issues… and for such keen, clear and easy collaboration towards *At*'s first poem.

Thanks to David Caddy for final proof-reading.

I would also like to thank the following who have, in some way or other, contributed to my making *At*: Paul Besley, Angus Carlyle, Gerrie Fellows, Louis Goodwin, Rob Greenwood, Chris Jones, Brian Lewis, Robert Macfarlane, Charles Monkhouse, Boz Morris, Simon Panton, Tom Prentice, Mark Spray, Janet Sutherland.

And thank you to Nikki, my closest fellow negotiator of places…

www.ingramcontent.com/pod-product-compliance
Lightning Source LLC
Chambersburg PA
CBHW031637160426
43196CB00006B/450